New Business Guide

New Business Guide

Some Practical considerations involved for Christians starting a business

Grahame Scofield

and

Ian M. Arbon

RoperPenberthy Publishing Ltd
Horsham, England

Published by RoperPenberthy Publishing Ltd
PO Box 545, Horsham, England

Text copyright © Grahame Scofield and Ian M. Arbon

The moral right of the authors have been asserted in accordance
With the Copyright Designs and Patent Act 1988

First published in 2005

ISBN 1 903905 22 2

Cover design by Angie Moyler

Typeset by Avocet Typeset, Chilton, Aylesbury, Bucks
Printed in the United Kingdom by Bell & Bain Ltd, Scotland

Contents

Part I   Some practical considerations involved for Christians starting a business

Part II   The preparation and content of the Business Plan

Part III   Endpiece

Part IV   References

Foreword

'Full – time Christian Workers' is a title most commonly given to Missionaries or people who have left the secular workforce in order to 'work for God' either in an evangelical or a Christian teaching/Pastoral capacity.

It is sad, that in this, many Christians have missed the point of their walk with God and have failed to realise, as Christians, we are *all* in 'full – time Christian work'. We all have the responsibility of living out our faith in every aspect of our lives, thus, putting God first in all that we do. This can be very challenging in today's world of business. Christians starting out on this difficult road need to be aware of the challenges they will be met with in relation to principals, honesty, integrity and upholding good Christian morals. However, I believe that, if we honour God in these areas, then He also will honour us for doing so.

From my experience as a Christian in business, I have found that spending time alone with God is essential for maintaining a healthy, Spiritual walk and, also, spending time with family is vital in order to maintain strong and loving relationships. If we fail in these areas, where is the pleasure in a successful business? – If we are not continually aware of these matters, business success may come at great cost.

I can honestly say, through all the years that I was involved in business, I have found no hard and fast rules for success and being a Christian in business does not guarantee a successful business but it does guarantee guidance from God. – If we seek God, He will reveal to us the way we should go.

Having been approached to write this foreword for a book about 'Christians in business', I have pondered upon how I could provide some valuable input to help someone starting out in business as a Christian. I decided that the best advise I could give would be to I encourage you to read and take on board the following two verses which I have found to be particularly helpful and effective in my own life:

1. Proverbs Ch 3 v 5-6; 'Trust in the Lord with all your heart and lean not on your own understanding; in all your ways acknowledge Him and He will make your paths straight.'
2. Colossians Ch 3 v 23-Ch 4 v 2; Whatever you do, work at it with all your heart, as working for the Lord, not for men, since you know that you will receive an inheritance from the Lord as a reward. It is the Lord Jesus Christ you are serving. Anyone who does wrong will be repaid for his wrong, and there is no favouritism.

Masters, provide your slaves with what is 'right and fair, because you know that you also have a Master in Heaven. Devote yourselves to prayer, being watchful and thankful.

My prayer is that, through reading this book, you will be inspired to stand without compromise in your faith in God and learn how to survive as a Christian in the difficult and challenging world of business.

– Be prepared for heartache; be prepared for excitement; be prepared for a roller – coaster ride but, above all, be prepared to stand firm in God.

Eddie Stobart Senior
Founder and retired manager of successful
haulage company, 'Eddie Stobart Ltd'.

New Business Guide

Part I – Some practical considerations involved for Christians starting a business

1. Introduction

The fact of your picking out this book indicates that you have an interest in the subject matter. This may be either as a newcomer to the business scene or as an adviser or friend to those considering a start. This book is different from the many others available on this subject. It approaches the issues specifically from a Christian perspective. It makes certain assumptions on the reader, which, unless understood makes much of what follows incomprehensible.

These are the assumptions:

- God as creator is **involved** in all aspects of his creation, including the business scene.
- In Christ we have the ideal **model** for a Godly life, if we follow his way in our business and personal lives.
- Through God's Holy Spirit we can **receive** ongoing input for all we seek to accomplish in his name.

If you are not yet able to accept these assumptions, then there are a number of publications listed at the back which may help you to consider your response, including how to accept the Christian faith for yourself.

We start by making a clear distinction between the way a Christian will approach a business start-up. He or she will be:

- in **faith** that **God** will be involved from the outset
- under the **direction** of Jesus for purpose, policy and operations
- seeking a supernatural **enabling** from the Holy Spirit to enhance his or her natural gifts.

We will then aim to do the best we can but leaving the **outcome** to Him.

All this implies that we are not claiming just a general blessing from God for our endeavours, but active **involvement** in all the practical aspects of our daily lives, particularly in the business scene. This may seem to be radical for many for whom faith is a personal matter and

9

restricted to weekends, home or family and whose calls on a personal God are restricted to emergencies. However, we invite you to accept the practical help available in this guide not only as good business practice but also to enable you to discover God's **guidance** for yourself.

If your perception of God and of the Christian faith is based on a different understanding we hope you will still feel able to explore alternative experiences with advantage. It is a spiritual principle to *"test all things; hold fast to that which is good."* (1 Thess 5:21). As you explore further may you find God's goodness and truth for **your** own situation.

2. The Call

Starting a business is an act of creation. As such it commands the attention of the creator just as every seed that is sown or every person who is born. As with all new creation it should not be undertaken without purpose, or casually, or without adequate preparation. Throughout this guide we shall refer to the model of the seed, its conception, growth and fruiting. Just as it is irresponsible to plant seed without considering carefully what will be the outcome, even more so with an infant business it is irresponsible to get started without a clear call, careful preparation and nurture and with a clear goal ahead.

Many who approach the prospect of their own business do so for the wrong motives. They may be discontented with their existing situation and imagine that starting a business may resolve their problems. Unfortunately business start-ups are a great deal more difficult than most imagine them to be. They require a variety of skills, usually longer hours of work and certainly much higher personal risks for the individual. At the present time about a third of new businesses started in the UK are no longer in existence after two years.[1] Apart from the risk of failure, for a Christian there is the added responsibility to be a faithful steward of resources and to bring honour to the Kingdom of God.

Therefore the first aspect to be considered must be the nature of our call. In this section we consider how to approach it, how to identify it and how to hear God's plan for our particular situation.

In the New Testament the words *"to those who have been called"* appear a number of times. There is a sense of setting apart for a special task. In Acts 13:2, referring to Paul and Barnabas, it talks of *"setting them apart for the work to which I have called them"*. We need to hear a similar call from the Holy Spirit as we start our planning. This concept of being called is different from any sense of preparedness or achievement. We are called because we are willing to serve, not because we are trained or equipped. It is often the case that we may happen to be both. But it is the call that is essential, the training can come later.

This is in contrast to the world's view where many preparing to start a business are encouraged to undertake some form of self-analysis. The 'know yourself' technique is designed to point up your strengths and weaknesses. You can easily apply this yourself by asking your family and friends or, alternatively, apply to a specialist. The outcome is helpful in establishing the way you are perceived by others. But only you know whether your answers to their questions have true objectivity and only God knows your inner being and more important your full potential.

11

Many Christians will assess themselves against the conceptual image of a strong-minded, forceful individual, willing to accept what it takes in the pursuit of a clear-cut vision of success. However, this conventional image is flawed because it is based on self-reliance. We are not aiming to be self-reliant but are seeking reliance on God enriching our human talents so as to make them sufficient for His purposes. The hard truth is that *"God chooses what is foolish in the world to confound the wise"* (1 Cor 1:27). So He is perfectly well able to use those of limited natural talents to confound those who may appear to have all the skills and intelligence for the task. Summing up, we need to see this as a calling, given by God, and not an extension of our natural skills. God will certainly use our natural skills but in His way and purpose.

If we continue to feel a call to start a business, perhaps the next stage is to determine its nature and application. Many of us have aspirations to do what we perceive to be significant work, that is jobs which provide status, power, authority and particularly financial reward. However, God's plan is for all jobs to be done. So it must involve the larger percentage of us taking up creative work of manufacture, agriculture, husbandry and so on. The so-called 'service' industries are really a misnomer as all work should be seen as a service to others. We may have natural skills and aptitudes, 'talents' as they are called in Scripture, which can lead us to a specialisation. We may have a gift of invention which has given us clear ideas about things that would be useful. We may feel that we have something unique to contribute to the management of our society. Alternatively, we may feel that we ourselves could do better what we have already been doing for others. Whatever the motivation, the call needs to be a real call, strong enough to bear the test of implementation. Good ideas are plentiful, but for a call to start a business to endure it must have sufficient depth and certainty to enable us to overcome problems and discouragement. We need to reach the stage when we know we can do no other than put this to the test.

For the Christian this is still not enough. We may be bursting to go ahead. We also need to know that God is with us and will support us at this specifically crucial point in our lives. To know that God **can** do it is different from knowing that God **will** do it – in your particular situation at your particular time. This involves what many would define as 'guidance'. Guidance implies an interactive relationship whereby you seek God's counsel and hear from Him. Seeking is invariably in prayer, when you share your ideas, your visions, your enthusiasm with God and ask Him for a green light to proceed. The light can come from a direct word, prophecy, Scripture or often through Christian friends. At the start of the endeavour this first green light is vital so that we proceed on the journey in the right direction and at the right time. If we start our journey under God's guidance we are more likely to stay with Him when we find ourselves under pressure. If we don't start with Him there are usually a lot of retraced footsteps until we do.

Using our analogy of the seed, we have first sought to find out if it is the right seed and that now is the right season for planting. Now we must consider the environment in which it is to be planted – the soil, the climate and the conditions necessary for that small bundle of creative energy to start in growth under the best of all possible conditions.

3. Making a Start

We are considering businesses starting up under a multitude of varied conditions. We are thinking of matters of scale and experience. We are thinking of regional variations in many countries in the world. We are thinking of countries with developed national infrastructures and possibly those with virtually no infrastructure at all. Despite each apparent diversity there is one common denominator which applies in every case. That is the nature of the world scene to which we subscribe and into which we are to plant our seed. This is the climate into which any seed, irrespective of soil, will grow. The seed needs certain essential elements – light, moisture and heat, sufficient for the task. These are the God-given elements which enable all life to be sustained and they are a *"free gift of the creator"*. (Job 5:10). However, we know that God gives this to all unconditionally and *"the rain comes down on the good and bad alike"*. (Matt 5:45). We need to know what are the good conditions and then align ourselves with them.

Many consider the world of business as a single corporate whole, with many divisions and variations but intrinsically a single, separate entity to be set alongside the world of home and family and the spiritual world of our church life. Jesus himself divided all activity into two kingdoms, the Kingdom of Mammon and the Kingdom of God (Matt 6:24). Most of us have been used to equating the world of business, in which money is the chief regulator, with the world of Mammon and have therefore assumed that whilst the Kingdom of God can have an influence on this world for good, it has no great influence on most of our day-to-day business experience.

We do not have time to consider in any depth the origins of the world of Mammon, but briefly it belongs to the very earliest period of man's fallen nature. It relates to the concept of a deity other than God himself. We note that from these times there has been worship of a mother-god who claimed the power to nourish us with her milk. The very name 'Mammon' has its roots in the word 'breast' from which words such as mammals and mammary are derived. In many early religions the multi-breasted goddess is a common object of worship, leading to all sorts of fertility rites and festivals and taking us away from the God of Scripture.

In time, the milk of Mammon has come to be linked to the world of money. Money is now the drip-feed that nourishes society. It is not easy to comprehend what are the sources of much business endeavour or the real motives that cause us to strive in business and the goddess to whom we may ultimately pay homage. This worldly mindset is so strong that most of us Christians cannot even realise that it is present. We live in a world of what might be called '**virtual reality**' where that which is seen and that which is generally accepted, is **actually** unreal. It takes a large measure of humility and Godly wisdom to recognise that many of us have been working for the wrong side for most of our business lives.

The Kingdom of God and the Kingdom of Mammon were themes explicitly taught by Jesus (Matt 6:24). He did not mince His words when talking to His followers. It was He who said you cannot serve both. At the start of our new business venture we need to determine whom we shall serve, God or Mammon. As we shall see, it makes a fundamental difference to all our business planning and performance. We need to emphasise the distinctiveness of the two kingdoms. They are under different rulers, different rules, are in opposition to each other and ultimately only one will prevail. If we place our business into the soil of the wrong kingdom we may be highly successful in the eyes of this world, but when we stand at the gates of heaven we may find that all we have to bring has turned into dust and ashes.

Reverting to our example of the seed, even before we consider the condition of the soil we must accept the rule under which we will live. Is it to be God's climate of obedience to Word and Spirit, or is it to be Man's climate of self-endeavour, striving, power and success? Both Kingdoms have massive resources, both Kingdoms can bring fulfilment. It is in their eternal purposes and powers of endurance that they are distinctive. Many will argue that there is a tinge of godliness about every human endeavour done for good motives. Whilst this may well be true, it does not contradict Christ's teaching about the Ruler of this World, our need to be wise and not just clever, our tendency to be beguiled by downright lies and our propensity towards self – our own lives and lifestyle. Christ's word says only when we relinquish our own lives do we inherit this eternal life (Luke 9:24).

We are considering how we make a start in new business and we have been examining fundamentals using the analogy of climate. Now we know there are many climatic variations in the world and if you are living in a hot, dry climate you may be wondering how one can ignore the regional differences. But just as there are soil and seed for all climatic types and planting and tending methods which will enable all plants to flourish, so these variations are all the gift of one God. Christian business rules are universal for all types and conditions of man and irrespective of what are our natural giftings. Otherwise we could not truly worship a God whose declared nature is love and from whom perfect justice prevails. If you are in a so-called Third World environment, with only basic business skills, even so your principles for business need to be in harmony with these universal criteria.

Jesus taught in the parable of building a tower *"For which of you desiring to build a tower does not first sit down and count the cost?"* (Luke 14:25). Jesus is stating that a norm for success is good planning. This is a Kingdom principle applicable to God in creation and also to us. We are talking about preliminary planning, not the full-blown Business Plan, which we shall consider in Chapter 6. This preliminary planning for the Christian is like a soil analysis – is it going to support the seed? The soil into which we plant is composed of many elements, and all are necessary for balanced growth. Some are the building blocks – Nitrogen, Carbon, etc and some are the trace elements – Potash, Iron, etc. We might liken these to the personal attributes of the individual – the natural balance of strengths and weaknesses with which we are endowed at birth and which are influenced by our growth and environment.

For a good soil analysis we need to identify the best ingredients for success or failure. We might consider our performance in relation to the following:–

a)   Effective use of time
b)   Attitude to money
c)   Ability to accept risk
d)   How we handle stress
e)   Having problems of control
f)   Ability to get on with others

If we honestly and prayerfully consider these aspects on a rating of say one to ten then we can get some idea of our strengths and weaknesses in areas of particular significance to starting a business. If in any area we rate ourselves under five, then we need to be aware of our weakness and consider how it might be corrected. We need to be very honest with ourselves. A low mark does not indicate failure but it may indicate that we are not yet ready for the particular endeavour of starting a business.

Having considered attitudes, we might next review what we have done in our lives, what has been achieved, what has gone wrong and particularly what we feel we could achieve given the right conditions. This may involve setting down details of your natural skills, your specialisation, what we might say is 'our subject' and considering it objectively as a contribution to the society to which we relate. If it were to be planted out under ideal conditions, would the flower and the fruit be something that we could offer wholeheartedly to God and His people as a blessing?

Above all, would our lives be fulfilled as a result, more than by doing many other good things but within a team led by others?

As our jottings take shape so we will want to define our ideas in more detail, particularly if they are product- or service-oriented. We need to consider what exactly we are proposing to provide, into what market it will go, whether there is a need or a niche, where our competitors will stand in relation to our plans. Especially we need to consider costs and prices to determine from the outset that there is the potential for a cost-effective end result. We are still talking of principles and not a full Business Plan. However, it is amazing how many people start out without a clear idea of what they plan to do, what it will involve and whether it will be cost-effective. Such endeavours, whether in the world of Mammon or in the Kingdom of God, will not find favour and lead to disappointment and failure. It is well to remember that God is not waiting to bless our plans, particularly if they are sloppy or not thought through. He will be prepared to influence plans carefully and prayerfully which are offered first to Him for His input and guidance. When we are in this relationship even our weaknesses and former failures can be transmuted by His strength.

So we have defined our seed, considered the climate and soil in which they will grow. If this results in an inward peace, we now have the encouragement to make a start. We will have given our preliminary plan our best effort as we have started in prayer what we have received will be wisdom and not just knowledge. We are now ready to do the sowing.

4. Sowing the Seed

For those who have a practical disposition, the preliminaries may have seemed to be a trifle tedious. In the parable of the sower (Matt 13:2), Jesus taught that the seed will only yield a harvest if it goes into good soil; anything else is no good. Jesus specifically attributes the stony ground to those who hear the word but let it fall away. He defined the weeds which choke the seed as the worry and illusions of this world's riches. We must be on our guard lest we allow these intrusions to influence our own sowing. Note especially that seeking after worldly success is like a thistle that will choke out the fruitfulness for the Kingdom.

Jesus also refers to the grain of mustard seed (Luke 13:8) which, being the smallest of seeds, grows into a great tree to shelter and protect. God's view of size is very different from that of the world. If you are a small enterprise you can still grow into something effective for the Kingdom. This leads us to examine the scale of our preliminary endeavour. There are two basic forms of business organisations: 'incorporated' and 'unincorporated'. If you are an individual just starting, the probability will be that you will start in the small-scale owner/proprietor category; this is an unincorporated type business known as a 'sole trader'. If you are sharing the vision with others you can still have an unincorporated business but it is then known as a 'partnership'. If you are planning to employ others, or take on an enterprise already formulated, then a corporate structure is perhaps necessary. There are two main types of incorporated business: a 'private limited company' and a 'public limited company'. In the former, all shares are owned privately and are not normally traded; in the latter, some or all of the stocks and shares are available for unconnected individuals and organisations to own and these are freely traded on a 'stock exchange'. It is worth noting that if you require any form of external funding, e.g. from Institutional and/or Trade Investors, your company must be incorporated. It is possible to consider the various pros and cons of each situation. However, as the regulations will vary widely between nations perhaps it is best to keep to general observations and commend the study of the details to the local situation.

Here are some considerations that you need to weigh prayerfully:

1. It is usually best to start in the simplest fashion. This is because it is less costly and it is relatively easy to change status upwards rather than downwards.
2. There may be a norm for your situation which your customers would expect. If you are dealing all the time with corporate customers a

corporate status will probably be appropriate for a new enterprise.

3. Only be willing to be joined in partnership with those you can trust. For Christians there is also the rule about uneven yoking (2 Cor 6:14).

4. Do not be persuaded to adopt a higher profile than you can sustain in practice. God does not appreciate pretenders and it is the way of Mammon to claim to be what you are not.

5. Never let considerations of taxation or personal wealth dictate how you should run your business. You are to be a faithful steward of the Master's treasure. He will tell you how and where it is to be distributed. Jesus paid his taxes on time and in full (Matt 17:24). As far as we know, He did not spend much time in tax planning.

This leads us on to the important matter of advice. The time that we sow is when we need good advice. We need to know what are the options and what effect will they have on our business. We need to secure the best advice at an acceptable cost. We need to know who will stay with us like a midwife during the delicate formative months whilst we are weaning our infant business. Grahame Scofield has been an adviser for new business for some twenty years. Before that he was involved in many new company starts usually as Chief Executive or Group Development Director. So he has a habit of proffering advice almost before it has been sought. However, in recent years he has come to recognise that much of this advice was based on the principles of a Kingdom from which he had withdrawn. When he committed his life and business to the Kingdom of God he drew a line under what had gone before and started a new learning process. It has taken **him** years to realise that he did not know the relevant guidelines! Hence, he is now much more diffident about offering advice and much prefers to seek advice before the Lord together with those he is advising, rather than offering an opinion.

So in the Kingdom start-up situation we would say that you need Kingdom advisers. Seek those who have gone before. They may not have the latest knowledge, not the best marketing methods, but they will have the mind of Christ and that is what counts. If you need to know where to find such people you could do no better than seek them out from amongst the ranks of International Christian Chamber of Commerce members worldwide (see section IV for address). The qualification for membership is that we have made the Lordship of Christ our primary business aim. Most of us have learned the practical way about Kingdom business and for some this has involved a complete change of direction. Your adviser needs to have the profile of a fellow traveller who is prepared and willing to take you by the arm and point you in the direction you should be going. He will not do this primarily for reward, although it is appropriate to pay for good advice. He will want to see your business flourish and will delight in the fruit that you produce.

Your adviser will usually be a source for obtaining information on the many practical steps involved in getting started. He usually can take care of the registration process, deal with the statutory bodies in respect of Income Tax, Corporation Tax, Payroll Tax, Value Added Tax (VAT), local state taxes and so on. He will also register a company or corporation and deal with business names, copyright, patents and so on. It is helpful to know which of these is going to be relevant in the initial stages and what will come later. You should not spend much time learning about things not essential at the preliminary stage. You need to conserve all time and energy for the actual start, rather than spending lengthy periods learning about procedures.

Having said this, a brief note of caution about Taxation. If you are not knowledgeable in this field, endeavour to become so. The old adage that "ignorance of the law is no defence" is never more true than of Taxation! No matter how well you believe your business to be doing, the Inland Revenue, and in particular the VAT authorities, will not hesitate to close down your business if they believe that you have insufficient funds to pay their bills.

Many people who have a skill in a particular discipline, say marketing, tend to overcompensate in the areas where they perceive themselves to be weak. Often this is seen in the desire to purchase a computer and to have the latest skills in financial management, whilst the business may only be raising a handful of invoices a month which could easily be recorded in a simple cash book. The converse is also seen. That is a disregard for that which is considered inessential, perhaps a concentration on sales, which ignores cash flow or proper recording. Both alternatives are likely to result in disappointment as we shall see when we look at the next subject.

5. Finance

Because finance is such a key element in any new business, a whole chapter will be devoted to it. Using the analogy of the planting, if we have the place and the time right and plant in good soil, finance might be considered to be the fertiliser. Its application is favourable for balanced growth. Too much or too little are detrimental and can be life threatening. We all know that Jesus taught a great deal about money; some say that apart from the nature of the Kingdom of Heaven it was His single most recorded subject. For that reason alone it must be important for disciples of His Kingdom to pay particular attention to all He says about money. Jesus once told a parable about those who were worldly-wise having more acumen than the faithful (Luke 16:5). Let us review what we have understood about the Kingdom, about money, about right stewardship and generally about the financial aspects of Kingdom business.

We may set down a series of propositions based on Scripture as follows:

1. Jesus told us to be faithful in the unrighteous world of Mammon – the world view of business, commerce and money systems as we have come to know them, **then** He would entrust us with true riches (Luke 16:11).
2. He described life in the Kingdom of God in many parables with an emphasis on talents and stewardship (Matt 25:15).
3. For Jesus, money was not a key issue. He used monetary resources when it was needed: to buy food, to pay taxes, hire a donkey, rent the upper room and to aid the poor. He had those around who saw it as their calling to minister to Him, presumably using their own financial resources (Matt 27:55).
4. The Pharisees tried to tempt him with various monetary devices: paying taxes to Caesar (Matt 22:17), paying the temple tax (Matt 17:24). Jesus taught about the good Samaritan (Luke 10:29), the widow's mite (Mk 12:41), using the Temple precincts as a market (Jn 2:14) and laying up treasure in heaven (Matt 6:19).

Financial transactions for Jesus were primarily a means of enabling His ministry, neither more important nor less than this. Before we claim that we do not have enough or that we can only proceed on a guaranteed balanced cash flow we need to be clear what we need to do. Conversely we cannot just ignore monetary considerations and say, as some do, "the Lord will provide!" and then find He may not. Nor can we take the approach that invites the Kingdom into the planning process and then invites the bank manager into the implementation process, unless of course he happens to be a Christian brother!

The approach which seems to be both Scriptural and practical might be set out as follows:

1. First count the cost, i.e. take stock of your opening position, what you think you can achieve in sales, what are your necessary start-up costs, what your cost of sales and overheads will be. This will give you a profile for your basic working capital. This must be done on a **cash** basis to allow for the time that sales will be converted to receipts and to allow for any prepayable expenses, such as insurance.

2. It is helpful to put this on a spreadsheet, either on paper or on a computer so that you can see the picture over a period, say six months to a year. We are not yet concerned with five-year plans as we normally do not have enough hard data to make these worthwhile. Pretty pictures can be made without much thought, but dependable information is of a different order.

3. Then, remembering the texts that refer to stewardship and ownership and reward we need to be realistic about entering figures for living expenses, tithes and a store for the future. If we base our own cash claims, be they wages, salary, drawings, spending money or however we describe them on what are our needs then we have a basis on which to work. Needs include provision for taxes and personal expenditure and will vary from person to person. They might include such items as a debt repayment profile, school fees, pensions, holidays and so on if these commitments need to be met.

4. The matter of tithing is really a subject in itself. The tithe in the Old Covenant was for a tenth of our net incomings. Jesus in the New Covenant did not set a tithe but likened us to agents of the King to whom we rendered our accounts. Such advice can hardly be ignored. Whether tithing or giving we need to set aside an appropriate amount, firstly to return thanks and then to provide for the needs of the Kingdom.

We are now at the point where a preliminary financial appraisal can take place. We can set down the figures for receipts and expenditure, including tithes or gifts and personal cash. This should produce a profile something like that at Appendix A and will show a gap between inflow and outflow. Most businesses need some form of cash injection to get them started. This is not necessarily an adverse feature as it usually relates to timing adjustments, principally as follows:

1. Some things need to be bought to start with – plant, equipment, tools, maybe a car or computer. Some of these can be leased but some may need to be bought outright.
2. There is a time delay between the moment of obtaining an order, for processing it, despatching it and receiving payment. This is the business cycle and often is the major ingredient of working capital. In working out what is a probable cash flow, due allowance needs to be made for suppliers who will only trade for cash and for customers who may be slow payers. In our experience, not being able to allow for customers who do not pay on time is one of the biggest single reasons for failure in small businesses.
3. Provision also needs to be made for contractual payments for wages, rent, etc and also any statutory liabilities, e.g. taxes. These should be planned to be paid on their due dates.
4. The difference between receipts and payment is the net cash flow. If you are starting with funds in hand this sum can be entered as opening capital and a projected monthly cash movement can then be derived. If you start with nil, the highest peak of resultant outflow will indicate the initial working capital requirement of the business.

As already indicated, it will be usual for a new business to have a working capital requirement. If this is very large the sums should be reworked so as to give a more realistic figure. To set out with a plan for working capital in excess of sales would tend to indicate something unusual! A few businesses can generate cash from the first month and you may of course be the fortunate exception.

Having established the working capital need, decisions need to be taken as to how this is to be found. Your adviser, who will have seen many similar situations, is often tempted to give you an immediate opinion! However, this is just where you need your Christian counsellor, who should remind you that the plan is not yours but is the Lord's. Particularly in the area of interface between the Kingdom of God and that of Mammon we need Godly wisdom. We advise you to seek to counsel in prayer, either alone or with family and Christian business colleagues. Above all, include your spouse if you have one in these times of prayer. It is God's plan that husbands and wives act together and in doing so we avoid all manner of dangers in the days ahead. It is safe to say that if you cannot share business issues at husband and wife level, then you probably cannot be in Kingdom business. This does not mean that you are looking for equal contribution and equal understanding of business issues, but it does involve a commitment to stand together in the business formation and agreement to pray and protect one another when the inevitable pressures arise. The classic Scriptural example of this husband and wife partnership in Christian business is the story of Aquila and Priscilla. We encourage you to study this together with your spouse (Acts 18:2,18,19,26; Rom 16:3; 1 Cor 16:19; 2 Tim 4:19).

So having brought our plan before the Lord we now pray for God's input into the plan. What exactly does this mean and how does it work? We know what our first rough position indicates. What we now need to know is how it can be refined and what is the right framework of our need. Then we need to seek the Lord for the right method of financing. How does God speak? Sometimes directly or by picture, most times by putting His inspiration into our minds, which brings into focus some ideas which were not there before. Some people will claim this is imagination, but holy imagining or meditation based on Scriptural principles is the very root of our Christian heritage. We need to get used to the idea of God planting his purposes into pliant hearts and for us to know when He has done it. There is nothing odd or unreal about this. It is God's Scriptural way, so it would be odd if it were not so. As we receive, so we can refine the plan and bring it closer to birth. This invariably gives rise to excited anticipation.

What happens if God does not speak? Then perhaps His answer is 'no', which is always difficult to receive. Perhaps it is 'not yet', or perhaps He has decided on another means of personal provision for this year and we are not minded to listen. God promises in His word to answer all who call upon him (Ps 3:4) and the problem in hearing is invariably with us.

When we have received guidance, the next most important thing is to write it down and then apply it. There is no good at all in reaching this point and then missing the way. It is like receiving from a rich man the key of his house and then promptly losing it. If the wisdom relates to actions or figures or alternatives it is necessary to rework the plan to match the guidance received. Often the guidance will have refined the figures, but a residual financial shortfall will still remain. This does not indicate a lack of prayer or of faith or that God cannot help. It means that we are now at liberty to consider established channels of resources, but with the King's blessing. We can find ourselves in a spiritual muddle over the goods of the world. The scriptures say that they are in the hands of the Prince of this world (Jn 14:30), but also that all of creation belongs to God (Ps 24:1). So if He gives us liberty to use the world's goods and provided we do so on His conditions then we can expect His support and covering.

We believe that the conditions that God imposes for us to be allowed to use the goods of the world may be summarised as follows:

1. Ask first, only proceed if you are at peace with the answer and have tested it with other Christians.
2. Borrow only what you need, and can see your way to repay.
3. Borrow from those within the Kingdom first if this is possible. In this way you can bless the lender by keeping his assets within the Kingdom and by giving him a fair return on his 'talent' of money.
4. If you do borrow from the world, do so only with reputable institutions, who are the normal providers of funds. This includes other businesses, banks, venture capital organisations, etc. Unless there are compelling reasons to do so, do not go to those at the speculative end of the money market, e.g. so-called 'business angels'.
5. Be aware that any investment by others in your business will be seen by them as risky. Banks, in particular, are not normally willing to **risk** money in your venture and so will make a repayable loan against appropriate security. Their first task is to secure their depositors' funds, not to make uncertain advances. Security may be in the form of a 'floating charge' over your business assets, or against your home, or a personal guarantee from yourself. Remember that you could lose everything you provide as security. Trade Investors and Venture Capital companies, on the other hand, are more likely to want a share of your business, i.e. an 'equity stake' and will expect to make their money from the eventual sale of shares.
6. Understand the terms of any loan and make a covenant before God to stick to these terms.
7. Remember that God's word in Proverbs applies regarding borrowing in the world. It puts you at the mercy of the lender and therefore subject to the ups and downs of world markets and economic pressures (Rev 22:7).
8. In ICCC we are believing for Christian lending institutions who are under the rule of God and who will operate exclusively under Godly principles. When these come along Christians should make a switch into these sources of funds (see also section IV).

Before we leave the subject of finance we need to think a little more about stewardship. We have assumed that our new business is to be under the government and lordship of Christ. So in effect He is the proprietor,

25

Chairman of the Board or whatever is the appropriate title. However, He is not the chief shareholder – not directly anyway. He has given us talents of time, energy, experiences and sometimes money. These are what He expects us to invest in the business. If you ask for a bank loan the bank will expect equal commitment from you so as to share the risk. Likewise God expects you to put in all your effort and resources into the operation so that He can put in His all alongside. Many have reservations about committing their own funds, or guarantees, or resources, but are quite willing to see others do so. We need to find the right balance between too cautious an approach and recklessness. God expects from us 100% commitment; anything less is going to be insufficient.

Before leaving the subject of finance there is one common problem area which is often more the result of misunderstanding than default. This concerns the concept of 'the business', which varies enormously depending on whether or not it is incorporated. Many newcomers to the world of **self**-employment (i.e. an unincorporated business) view the business as somehow detached from themselves, almost having a life of its own. It is not uncommon to hear remarks such as 'the business' can afford it or 'charge it to the business' as though somehow there is a third party involvement and the owner or proprietor is detached from the transaction. It needs to be emphasised that, in its unincorporated form, 'the business' does not operate independently, cannot think for itself, and most certainly does not owe you a living. Anything charged to the business is merely a transfer from one pocket to another. If you cannot afford it, the business is unable to cover the gap, unless of course you choose to borrow from your creditors, which, apart from being unethical, usually leads to problems. Finance for personal needs is best dealt with by firstly staying within your plan and secondly monitoring your plan on a regular basis to establish just what you can afford.

This is one of the main reasons why companies incorporate. A corporation **is** a legal entity, separate and distinct from its owners and is most certainly not synonymous with you as a Director. Corporations can borrow money and own property, can sue and be sued and can enter into contracts. As a Director, you will be an employee of the company, which **can** be said to operate independently, think for itself and may well owe you a living! One of the most common mistakes in private limited companies is to confuse the roles of 'director' and 'shareholder', especially when you may be both simultaneously. In our experience in the UK, too many people aspire to the Director title but are blithely unaware of the awesome responsibilities in law that are carried by Directors of even small businesses.

6. Developing your Business Plan

Chapter 5 has dealt with the preliminary planning of the business and we have hinted several times that this will usually lead to the development of a full-blown Business Plan. If, as is usually the case for anything but the smallest of business ventures, you are looking for external investment, a professional Business Plan is one of the first things a potential investor will look for. Indeed, the lack of a plan, or a plan of poor quality, is most likely to result in an off-hand rejection of any application for funds.

Equally, if you are already in business and require finance for capital projects, new product development, acquisitions, management buyouts, working capital or to start a new venture, banks and financial institutions will expect you to have first drawn up a Business Plan.

So what is a Business Plan, and how is it prepared? What should it achieve and how does it best do so? What value does it have for the managers of a business? These are the questions we shall seek to answer in this chapter.

Importance of Your Business Plan

Business is a highly creative activity which requires a broad range of skills and qualities. To start and develop an enterprise successfully will need more than just the expertise involved in operating a particular venture, even with a good measure of hard work, dedication and commitment.

If the enterprise is of any size you will find yourself proportionately dependent on the skills and knowledge of others. The role of the entrepreneur or chief executive may be seen as the controlling of a multiplicity of ingredients, ensuring that they blend and function cohesively and effectively. A good Business Plan is an essential tool in achieving those aims.

Possessing a good Business Plan is no guarantee of success nor of avoiding failure. The cause of failure is often that owners and managers did not anticipate quite simple factors which could have been foreseen. These may include misunderstanding the market, not having enough money or lacking clear aims and objectives.

By itself, a Business Plan will not overcome any of these common faults. However, the process of formulating one, and of having to expose calculations and assumptions to detailed formal scrutiny, can ensure that weak points are identified early enough to make positive changes. A business plan may also aid in clarifying and crystallising thinking, providing milestones and goals and giving a business direction and focus.

A Business Plan is most frequently used as a means of attracting investment from outside sources, whether equity or loan capital. It explains the enterprise in detail, so that investors may judge whether it is one worth backing. For those about to set up a new enterprise, it is never too early to start preparing your Business Plan. For those who have been going for some years, it is never too late to begin.

Twin Tasks

We thus see that the Business Plan fulfils two main tasks. It acts as a 'selling' document to investors and other outside bodies, and as an aid to management. The external bodies might include your bank, important suppliers, licensors, and arms of local and central government from which you may obtain grants and loans or Trade Investors and Venture Capital companies who will consider taking an equity stake in the business. For unincorporated businesses and those whose businesses are not complex, an abridged version may be all that is necessary. But this cannot be done until full consideration has been given to all aspects of the Plan.

There is no such thing as a uniform Business Plan – just as there is no such thing as a uniform business. Potential providers of finance would regard a standard Business Plan, looking exactly like hundreds of others, as describing a standard business, as one unlikely to possess the fresh, vital and dynamic qualities that will make it a thriving success.

Your business is different, which is why it will be that much more successful than others competing for the same investment money. Your Business Plan must express that unique quality, as well as capture the fire and enthusiasm you feel for it. If you have been following the first five chapters of this book and have completed your preliminary plan, you will also have the assurance that your business is God-inspired and in accordance with His will. Preparing your Business Plan should be a spiritual exercise along with all that has gone before it.

While every Business Plan must aim to be different, there are some rules it is wise to follow.

Professional Advisers

Your professional advisers, usually your accountants, should be able to help in a number of ways. They can:

- Introduce you to a range of potential investors
- Advise on different types of finance available
- Help crystallise your ideas for the plan
- Develop an appropriate layout and structure

- Prepare and appraise financial projections
- Review the contents and presentation of the plan
- Identify weaknesses and inconsistencies
- Advise on what you may realistically expect from investors.

Who Should Write the Plan?

Business Plans are rarely completed in a single draft; indeed, they are constantly redrafted, which is why it is advisable to use a proprietary word processing package in the preparation. However, the final version should preferably be the product of one person, however much help he, or she, may receive with technical and financial details.

If you are the owner, or senior partner, in the enterprise, it is sensible to take responsibility for the task. When it comes to answering detailed questions from potential investors about aspects of the plan, it will not help your case to have to reply that you didn't write that section.

Research

As the plan will cover almost every aspect of the business, it is advisable to start collecting the information that may be helpful over a number of weeks, or even months. As you come across material that may be useful, store it, or write down ideas as they occur to you. If you have done your preliminary planning, see chapter 5, this will automatically be the case.

If you are starting a new business, you should find this research helpful. Existing businesses will already have a lot of the data but finding it may take time.

Outline of the Plan

Divide your research into the different categories that will comprise the final version. You may, of course, decide later to use more, or fewer categories. Ensure there is a logical flow of information through the various sections. Put yourself in the position of someone wanting to find out about a business. How would you like the information to be presented?

The number, and even the position, of the sections will depend upon the size and nature of the business. In Part II of this book, we have provided you with a very detailed outline of a Business Plan. The outline is not infallible and rigidly following it will not guarantee that you will obtain the requisite funding for your business. It is, however, an outline born out of many years of experience of writing Business Plans and has been actually used to successfully obtain funding for start-up businesses. It is a detailed plan and may be more than needed for a simple enterprise. However, by considering the various headings and adapting the content for your own circumstances even the simplest of situations can be improved.

Presentation
Having expended valuable time and effort in writing your Business Plan, don't let it be undersold by poor presentation. But don't go to the other extreme and make it too lavish a publication. A glossy printed booklet would suggest unnecessary waste and extravagance and investors might become fearful about how you would spend their money. Given the huge advances in desktop publishing software over the past few years, it is possible to produce a very professionally-presented Business Plan quite inexpensively.

A well-produced and laid-out document is what the recipients expect. Don't try to cram too much on to the page – but don't let it run to too many pages either. Between 20 to 50 pages, depending on the scale and nature of the business, is recommended; a thick document can be off-putting to the recipient. Use charts and graphics to illustrate and help simplify complicated information but only when it achieves that purpose.

Essential Features
The essential features of a good plan are:

Marketing
- Production dates
- Adopt a marketing approach – you are marketing your business
- Show your and/or your management's enthusiasm and commitment
- Demonstrate your understanding of the business
- Indicate your company's growth prospects
- Highlight the unique features of your business

Readability
- Write to hold the reader's interest
- Be concise – don't bore readers with too much detail
- Keep the appropriate length
- Pay attention to presentation as well as content
- Use visual aids where appropriate

Feasibility
- Don't be over-optimistic
- Highlight challenges, showing how they will be met
- Cover all the key areas of your business.

Recipients

Who you approach for money, and thus to whom you send your Business Plan, obviously depends on the type of business it is and what kind of money you seek. A mature business in a mature industry with strong assets looking for a mixture of preference and equity investment would seek a different channel from a high-risk start-up company.

Your advisers should be able to suggest names of organisations that invest in firms such as yours.

You may worry about giving out a large amount of confidential information concerning your business. If you are anxious, it may be sensible to send just the summary first. Mark it 'Private and Confidential', and indicate that it is '©' copyright material.

The Business Plan is often an interface between your Christian vision and its practical implementation. If it is addressed to those outside the Kingdom then it should be in words and form that they can comprehend. Such statements as 'God told me...' may be true but are unlikely to be properly understood. Conversely, a commitment to Christian ethical standards would be understood and accepted.

Reactions to Business Plans vary widely, often depending on the circumstances of the lender, the general economic climate and the number of applications under consideration. A negative initial reaction does not always mean that the Plan is no good. It will need to be reconsidered and any comments received carefully weighed. Often a Plan will secure favour on the second or third approach.

7. Tending the Young Growth

So far we have considered the criteria for making a start, the method of getting started, the right time, soil and climate. We have considered the financial needs and the appropriate dosage of fertiliser that will bring growth. We have prepared a detailed Plan of the way ahead. If all the steps have been followed faithfully and all indicators are still positive, now is the time to make a start. With much prayer plant the seed and allow God to bring the increase (1 Cor 3:6).

In this chapter we consider the young growth, how to tend it and ensure that it makes ideal progress. This implies that the new growth will be regularly inspected, measured and generally given close attention, just like a new baby being brought into the home. It may just happen that the seed for some reason just does not take. Any gardener will tell of the unexplained disasters with favourite seeds. All that can then be done is to go back to the start and commence a new plan. Likewise the growth may be so weak for reasons that are readily apparent that it may be better not to proceed further. These may be emotive decisions but we are looking for fruitfulness, not stunted growth.

Assuming the growth is as expected we need quickly to measure performance and chart progress. This is usually done with a bookkeeping system that can record the basic elements of sales, costs and overheads and so produce a profit report. Slightly more information will enable you to do a cash flow report. All of this information can be combined into a statement of wealth or net worth, often set out in the form of a Balance Sheet. In this brief account there is insufficient space to consider the merits of manual or computer records, the multitude of proprietary systems and the variety of issues to be considered which depend on the type and scale of the organisation. All these can be explained by your adviser who should be able to provide practical experience of alternative systems and discuss with you what you require.

There are many good reasons why you should set up a good recording system, and learn how to use it. Firstly, numeracy is a fact of life in business. If you have to rely on others to understand your own business you are hardly in control of your affairs. It will be a weakness which you will have cause to regret. Conversely if you make a point of learning the basics so that you can enter your own data and interpret your own results you reap a number of benefits.

1. You can interpret your results and take appropriate steps rather than wait for others.

2. You can act as a backup to systems so as to ensure continuity and security.
3. You will know where you are with customers, suppliers, the bank and yourself, rather than leaving the interpretation to others.

As your business grows it may be necessary to delegate this bookkeeping function. However, the ability to navigate around your own system will be invaluable and is to be recommended even when updates to the systems become necessary.

Having secured the information, the second most important step is to interpret what you have secured. To have got this far, you will already have produced your Business Plan which will have included detailed spreadsheets of how you expected your business to perform in the first twelve months. Now is the time to measure **actual** monthly performance against this plan. Some like to call the plan a budget. We prefer to define the budget as something you have a reasonable expectation of achieving. In the very early stages of a business this is rarely a certainty, therefore we prefer the word 'plan' or 'forecast'. A comparison of actual performance with the plan will throw up a number of variations, or 'variances' as they are sometimes called. These can be measured either in absolute or in percentage terms, i.e. sales up by £5,000 or 10%. At every level these variances are important as they show the trend the business is taking. Key performance variances are firstly the difference between total earnings and total measured costs, known as the net profit or surplus, and secondly, the measure of cash flow between what has happened and what was expected. It must be emphasised that for a number of reasons, in the short term, these measures may not run together. Evidence of the availability of cash may be an indication of profit, but is not necessarily so; it may indicate that customers have paid in advance or that bills are still due for supplies already received.

The interpretation of results is a skilled business. Usually when we are growing seeds for the garden we would not consider taking them to the plantsman for a check. At the other extreme it would be rare not to take a new-born infant for a regular check-up. A new-born business also needs a regular external check-up. This check-up will consider the trend of the figures but also review a number of other matters which cannot be quantified in figures. Accountants often have a complex about figures; they give undue prominence to those they see, forgetting that they are not the only key organisational indicators. The old usage of the word 'auditor' as one who hears an account of a business venture is more in line with what is required.

A good adviser will want to hear about you and the business, your perceived view of progress, your aspirations and problems. Then he will discuss the figures with you. Jointly you will identify any opportunities that can be taken or corrections that need to be made. Any problems will be recorded. These matters will then be taken up in prayer, either at the time or with a group of committed Christian colleagues. This is a two-way matter – us giving our Master an account of our stewardship and our hearing from Him concerning His plans and expectations. This is one of the strengths of the local groups of ICCC members when they meet together on a regular basis.

You can see that if this aspect of the new business is neglected, not only are you very much on your own, but you miss those most central attributes for Christian fellowship with one another and supremely fellowship with God. It is just amazing how many Christians in business would pray for the nation, for the Church, for the sick and needy, for their own family, but when it comes to their business this is an area where they are either in defeat, or have persuaded themselves that God is not into computers or banking or credit control or manufacturing or whatever aspect of the business world they find themselves in. And they are probably correct. God never intrudes unless He is invited. If we keep our businesses to ourselves and consider they are 'off limits' to Him, so they will be. However, as we shall see in our next section on fruitfulness this can have serious consequences for our long-term health.

8. Fruitfulness

Every seed has a specific objective built into its genetic code. If it is a flower it is to flower and produce fresh seed. If it is a vegetable, it is to produce wonderful vegetables. If it is a fruit, to produce delicious fruit. So with a new business it needs to have an objective in view so that it can mature and come into its own fruitfulness. These objectives are often very hazy at the outset. Many Christians have a perception that their business should in some way serve the Lord without ever bothering to establish how, or to measure whether they are achieving what they set out to do, or indeed whether God is pleased with the result.

Perhaps the most common reason given for starting a Christian business is that there is a desire to make money to serve the Kingdom. This apparently laudable objective is often the result of a much more self-centred thought process which goes something as follows: if I commit my spare money to the Lord then the Lord is bound to bless my business and incidentally I will prosper and receive self-esteem. The result is usually disaster. God sees the intentions of our hearts (Ps 44:21). He is not fooled by pious statement of intent. He does not need our money, so why should He make our lives comfortable when, usually, spiritual growth comes from endurance and overcoming adversity.

So what should be the goals of Christians who want to put their businesses under the direction of the Lord? The best way to find out is to ask. The best place to search is in the Scriptures and the best place to receive vision is to join up with others who are travelling on the same road. The book of Proverbs is a good place to start because it talks a lot about wisdom and the comparison between the ways of God and the ways of men. However it is primarily in the New Testament that Jesus exposes the distinctiveness of The Way and all that had gone before. He rejected both Jewish legalism and the Graeco-Roman emphasis of knowledge. His message was one of service, first to God then to mankind. There were no opt-out clauses and the greatest sin was that of selfishness. Jesus himself told us that the Prince of this World had been allowed domination over the world of man for a limited term (Jn 14:30). Satan had set about distorting truth which led to man seeking selfish ends. The greatest lie was that man was able to control his own destiny to do away with the need for a creator. The greatest distortion would be man made into the image of man.

A drip feed of the milk of Mammon has held the world in a poisonous grip. The evidence is to be seen if looked for. The world is in an unholy mess. The rich get richer and the poor get poorer. The environment for

35

which man is a steward is being destroyed. The power of the multinational exceeds that of the politician. Money has run out of control and is replaced by virtual money – which is not actually there but appears under funny titles such as 'derivatives' or 'futures'. Those who seem to be fair-minded and decent are rendered ineffective and power is in the hands of unseen shadow figures.

Jesus tells us to expect these things but not to join in (Matt 24:13). To be prepared for what lies ahead and come under his covering in the days of calamity. Now is not the time to go into considerations of the secrets of the end times. However, there has always been only one option for the Christian – to seek first the Kingdom (Luke 12:31) and this applies to Christians starting their own business as with any other. What then does it mean to seek first the Kingdom in the business context?

1. The first priority of the business is to proceed in whichever way God will reveal.
2. This must be achieved through following the rules of Kingdom living and not under worldly rules, be they conventional, economic or management.
3. The way in which priority will be achieved is unique for each business. It will be revealed step-by-step and it will harmonise into the plan for other Christians.
4. God will place a hedge around his Kingdom people and Kingdom business. In times of trial they will endure crisis but they will be protected and survive.
5. Their purpose will be to provide refuge for the needy and to support the work of the Kingdom just as it was in the days of Joseph when God predicted famine. His plan through Joseph was that the children of Israel would not starve. We see a parallel in our own days. The Christians in business are there not for themselves, not for the exploitation of their own talents, but for the Kingdom people in the days ahead.

So when we talk about fruitfulness, what we are really saying is that the fruit will be plentiful, of great variety and of excellent quality. It will not be for us alone but to share with all God's people. It will be a great harvest, some thirtyfold, some sixtyfold, some a hundredfold of what has been sown. This is the word of the Lord (Mk 4:3).

9. Conclusion

We have endeavoured to set out the distinctiveness of the Christian business start-up. We have tried to be radical, that is to get to the root of matters. If you are looking for a more traditional type of approach, there are a number of excellent text books listed in the appendix. Within ICCC we believe that we have a calling into the marketplace so as to demonstrate this calling and to push back the forces of Mammon. We have an immense task, transforming our minds from our own experience and assumptions into minds governed by God's Spirit. We need to heed prophecy and vision, dream dreams and believe the unbelievable. We believe that we can roll up a corner of the carpet of commerce to reveal the firm ground on which businesses can be founded. We believe this will be replicated across the world with country after country giving priority not to narrow self-interest but in encouraging others in the vision of these days.

All this will involve spiritual warfare. In ICCC we believe that it is so important that prayer takes an active place in our activities and planning that we are encouraging the appointment of **intercessors** for each business. They will be people who can be trusted, who are mature Christians, and who have a heart for supporting the ministry into the marketplace. The power of prayer gives us the strategic advantage as we deal with the world. We will invariably be Davids in the battle with Goliath but prayer can steady our aim so that the battle will be the Lord's.

If you would like to learn more about any of the matters set out in this booklet, there is a list of references in the appendix. Particularly, we would encourage you, if you are not already in touch, to contact an ICCC member who lives near you and to attend a meeting or business clinic. Then you will be able to meet people seeking to live out the business practices recommended in this book. They will be the ones, particularly at local level, who will encourage you to plan, make a start, review, grow and be fruitful for the glory of God and the building of His Kingdom in these days.

New Business Guide
Part II – The preparation and content
of the Business Plan

Section A	Executive Summary
Section B	The Company and its Industry
Section C	The Products/Services
Section D	Markets
Section E	Marketing
Section F	Design/Development
Section G	Manufacturing/Operations
Section H	Management
Section J	Implementation Schedule
Section K	Financial Highlights, Risks and Assumptions
Section L	Detailed Financial Plan
Section M	Items for Appendices

For each section there is a narrative describing the principles for completing the section. This is followed by a checklist of items to consider as it is being written. Both elements are important for a comprehensive Plan. We suggest you read a section, prepare a draft, consult the checklist and make additions and amendments.

All businesses need to consider all aspects of their formation, development and business environment. Whilst small businesses may not need to report in such detail, and while certain elements will not be applicable to service businesses, most businesses will have aspirations to grow. The discipline of considering all aspects of the business right from the start will avoid any confusion arising at a later stage.

Preparing the Business Plan is a spiritual exercise. Commit the endeavour to prayer before you start, during its implementation and particularly when you are preparing to submit it to your financial backers.

Section A – Executive Summary
Business Plan Content

This section appears first and summarises all that follows. It should be written last. Potential investors will read this part and often no further unless you can capture their interest and imagination. It is vitally important to get it right. Judgments will be made on the basis of an impression created in less than two pages of typescript.

It must be accurate and succinct, an informative but punchy description of all that you are doing and hope to achieve. Yet it must assume ignorance of your business and the industry or sector in which it operates.

Keep it businesslike, but as natural as possible. Avoid jargon, religious slogans and stilted commercial phraseology.

The Business
Describe your business, what it does and why it is different. State how long it has been going, how it started – or when it will start. Say what the market is and why it is attractive to you and potential investors.

Talk about your customers and who they are; what proportion of your output they account for and why they buy from you rather than your competitors. Who are your competitors and what advantages do your products or services enjoy that theirs don't? Is it quality, delivery, price, innovative features or something else?

What are the main achievements of your business? How quickly has the business evolved to its present position and size? Focus on its main strengths and weaknesses. Show that you are aware of areas where improvement is required – without giving them undue emphasis.

Management
People are as important as products and ideas. Describe the people in your business, starting with yourself if you are the owner or senior partner. List directors and, if important, managers and key employees. Briefly state their titles and responsibilities, how long they have been with the business and what relevant experience and qualifications they possess.

Indicate what they do, and how they relate to each other; if they have a stake in the business, say how much. If it is a new venture or if there is to be a major financial reconstruction, state what proportion of the shares they would expect to own. Include mention of share option schemes and any employee share scheme, existing or envisaged.

Financial Information

Provide basic financial information, such as sales or turnover, pre-tax profits, capital employed, etc, with a historical summary showing the growth of the business. Indicate what future growth is anticipated, from where, and what earnings may be expected. For all projections, indicate the period over which these will be achieved.

Investment

State in round figures how much money is required, and in what form. Will it all be equity investment, with the investors owning shares? Will some be loan finance, and if so what kind of security will be provided? What will be the ratio of debt to equity financing?

Say why you want the money, and what it will be used for: buying new plant and equipment, or developing new markets. Perhaps some is needed as working capital to finance raw material purchases, or for the holding of stocks. Estimate when it will be repaid, and how. Itemise in broad terms the risks and rewards for the investor.

Section A – Executive Summary
Business Plan Checklist

The executive summary should provide a brief overview of the plan. It is the most important section in that it may well determine the amount of consideration your proposal will receive by the potential investor. It must express succinctly the uniqueness and viability of your venture.

Recommendations
- Normally, the executive summary should be restricted to a maximum of two pages.
- Write it after the rest of the Business Plan is complete.
- Ask several knowledgeable business contacts to review the summary to test its effectiveness.

Key elements
Describe your business and why it is unique:

- What is your product or service?
- Why is your market attractive?
- Who are your customers?
- Who are your competitors?
- Why are your products or services preferable to those of your competitors?
- How far has your company evolved to date?

Briefly state management's qualifications:

- What is management's past success record?
- What abilities do management bring to the venture?
- How is ownership to be distributed?

Present your financial projections summary:

- How much growth is expected?
- What earnings are projected?
- Over what period of time will these be achieved?

Indicate the amount, form and use of finance:

- How much finance is required?

- What form will the funding take? (Equity? Debt?)
- What will the money be used for?
- How will finance be repaid?
- What are the risks/rewards for the investor?

Section B – The Company and its Industry
Business Plan Content

Now you can give information in more detail. But remember brevity is still necessary. Start with the business, when it began operating and who the founders were.

The Story So Far
Say what you were doing before, and what were the reasons and motives for starting up in business. Was it your idea, or that of a partner or colleague? Was it because you wanted to work for yourself? Or that you spotted a good opportunity and decided to exploit it? Are you a born entrepreneur, a self-made one or has it come about following redundancy or for other reasons?

State the present status of the business – a sole trader, partnership, co-operative, limited, unlimited or public company. If it is a company, state the date of incorporation, number of shares authorised and issued and to whom.

Did you start from scratch, or buy or inherit an existing business? Recall the original intentions and ambitions and say how they have changed as the business has progressed. Give what you consider to be the main accomplishments of the business so far and say what setbacks you have had – plus why you think they happened.

Make sure you include financial information in describing the development of the business, including how it is presently financed. Who owns the equity, and what loans, mortgages, overdrafts, debentures, etc. are outstanding?

Investors will probably possess only a general and somewhat hazy knowledge of the industry or sector in which you may have spent your working life. Tell them about it, or enough for them to be able to gauge the major developments and how you fit into the overall picture.

Critical Success Factors
This exercise can be among the most rewarding to you personally. Few ever sit down and actually think about where they fit into the industrial scheme of things. Industry in this context includes both manufacturing industry and service industry. It can improve your general perspective and understanding of how your industry operates.

State the current size of the industry in overall figures, such as value of sales, numbers employed, number of companies, etc. Who are the industry or market leaders? Is the sector dominated by a few, or is the

43

market fragmented? Are there a large number of potential customers or do a handful account for a high proportion of sales value?

Say something about factors that are important in your field. Can supplies or raw materials be a problem? Are there many or only a few suppliers, both in terms of the number of components or ingredients you use, and in the number of companies you buy from? If supplies are subject to disruption, spell out what sort of problems that would pose.

If sales are affected by the vagaries of fashion, say how frequently you need to change the product line. Indicate the proportion of revenues that has to be devoted to research and development, design and marketing, etc. Are there major environmental, technological or legislative factors that might change the commercial outlook? Quote published forecasts, if available, about future prospects and trends for the industry. Relate them to the particular segment in which you operate, and to the experience of your business.

Section B – The Business and its Industry
Business Plan Checklist

Rightly or wrongly, the potential investor will often evaluate the future potential of your business on the basis of past performance and a brief summary of the development of your business is therefore required. An outline history explaining how your business relates to other participants in the industry and what trends affect your industry gives the reader a basis upon which to evaluate your plans. If your business is fairly complex, it may be useful to evaluate the company and/or its industry using a 'PEST' analysis, or Porter's Five-Forces Diagram.

Key elements
Provide a history of the development of your business:

- Date and form of incorporation
- Who were the main founders?
- Present financing
- What are the major accomplishments of your business?
- What setbacks have you met?

Describe the industry in which you operate/wish to operate:

- What is the current size of the industry?
- Who are the major participants in the industry? (Competitors? Market leaders? Suppliers?)

i. What factors are important to success in your industry?
ii. If available, what do published forecasts say about the future growth and profile of the industry?
iii. Why are your products or services preferable to those of your competitors?
iv. What fashions, legislation or environmental trends affect your industry?
v. What are the 'barriers to entry' for your business in its chosen industry?

Section C – The Product or Service
Business Plan Content

What Is the Product or Service?

The text should flow logically into a full description of what it is that you actually make, or provide. Similar business principles apply to firms in manufacturing, sales and service industries, even though methods may alter.

Describe the physical appearance of the product or service, and what it does. Say what needs it fulfils, and how it is perceived by customers and by the industry. Above all, say what it is that gives your product its particular advantage or so-called USP (unique sales proposition): quality, technology, special features, availability, cost, etc.

If the product or service is highly technical in nature, do not give the reader too much detail. Save it for an appendix at the back. Say whether you have obtained or applied for patents or other protection. The specification may serve as an appendix.

Technology

State the stage of technical development the product has reached. Is it still on the drawing board, a working model, in production, or in use? Can the product range be expanded, and if so how, into what new areas and at what cost? If the purpose of raising money is to fund this activity, then highlight this aspect. Similarly, emphasise the purpose for which you need the cash – setting up the production facilities, for example.

Touch upon both specific (to you) and general aspects of technical developments. What are your objectives and how much will new technology and technical advances affect what you plan? How important is research and development to your business, and what will you need to spend? How much of your resources, both financial and human, will this demand?

Competition

Look, too, at what is happening outside. Who are your competitors, and how does your product or service compare with what they currently produce? What are their technological developments, and how will these affect you? Forecast the opportunities, pressures, or urgency for you to develop revised or second and third generation products.

Cash Considerations

Don't overlook the financial considerations. Explain your pricing policies both for products and services. If for products you need to define the level of stocks of raw materials and finished products you need to maintain, how goods are distributed, the pattern of sales and the frequency with and quantities in which goods are ordered. Talk about cash flow. By now your reader should be anxious to hear what you have to say about the market.

Section C – The Product or Service
Business Plan Checklist

You should provide a full description of your product or service, consider planned developments (although more detailed Design/Development should be dealt with in Section VI) and assess any competitive products (although detailed market surveys should be left for Sections IV and V). You should note that with the growing dominance of the Service sector, some companies describe 'Services' as 'Products'; for the sake of clarity, this should be avoided.

Recommendations
i.   Use charts where appropriate to compare your product with those of your competitors.
ii.   Include photographs or drawings if you think they are helpful.
iii. Do not make this section too technical – remember that the investor is unlikely to have your technical knowledge; if necessary attach an appendix.
iv.   Describe the advantages of your product.

Key elements
Fully describe your product or service:
i.   What need does it fulfil?
ii.   What features make it unique?
      (Cost? Technology? Versatility?)
iii. How is your product or service perceived in the industry?

Discuss the development of your product or service:
i.   How fully developed is your product or service?
      (Working model? In operation? In use?)
ii.   Are there opportunities to expand the product/service line?
iii. Is your product patented or otherwise protected by copyright? How easy is it to imitate the service you are providing?

Discuss competitive products on the market:
i.   How do they compare in quality and features with your product?
ii.   Why do customers buy the competitors' products?
iii. What pricing strategies are pursued for these products?
iv.   Is it normal to pay commissions or offer discounts?

Research and development:
i.   What are the future developments and objectives?
ii. Discuss the influence of new technology.
iii. What are the technical risks?
iv. Describe the state of your competitors' technological developments and how these will affect you.
v.   Consider second and third generation products.

Financial considerations:
i.   Explain your pricing strategy.
ii. Indicate the required levels of stocks of raw materials and finished products.
iii. What are optimal order sizes?
iv. How is distribution effected?
v.   Consider cash flow requirements.

Section D – Markets
Business Plan Content

What is the Market Opportunity?
Next to the summary, this is the section that will be read most closely. It could usefully be the part you prepare first, so that all else flows from it.

Unless a market exists for your goods or services, unless people in sufficient numbers are willing to part with money to obtain them, then you don't have a business. Show that a market does exist. Then point out the gap in it you have identified.

In doing so, demonstrate your understanding of market forces and how they work. Show that you are able to market your products effectively. Give a realistic estimate of what potential market share you believe you can obtain, quoting the assumptions you make in arriving at this figure.

Indicate that you have fully appraised the impact of competitors on the market. Show that you have neither overestimated your strengths nor underestimated your weaknesses.

Market Research
More research will be needed to describe the market, its size, history, stage of development, and expected growth rates. Obtain published data, such as surveys and forecasts. Quote these sparingly, but intelligently. Don't hide unfavourable factors, such as barriers to entry and other unusual characteristics.

Market Share
Give your present market share, if you have one, saying whether you expect to benefit from an enlarged market, or by taking business from your competitors. Describe your existing customers, where they are located and their sensitivity to price, quality or service. Also mention any market research that you have commissioned or obtained, and list reactions from those who have bought, tried or shown interest in your product.

Section D – Markets
Business Plan Checklist

In this section you should describe the opportunities available in your market and show how your proposals will exploit them successfully. It may be helpful to prepare this section of the plan first, since some of the other sections, such as operations and finance, will be dependent on the ability of your business to penetrate and expand in the market.

Recommendations
i. Show that a market exists for the products or services you will provide.
ii. Show that you understand the market forces and have the abilities and resources to supply and publicise your products effectively.
iii. Make a realistic estimate of your potential market share based on sound assumptions.
iv. Give a concise appraisal of the competition and do not overestimate your strengths or underestimate your weaknesses.
v. Use charts where appropriate to compare your company's strengths and weaknesses with competitors.
vi. Do not unjustifiably slight your competitors' abilities. Investors expect to obtain an in-depth understanding of why your sales goals can be achieved despite competition.

Key elements
Describe your customers:
i. Who are they? (Individuals? Manufacturers? End users?)
ii. Where are they located geographically?
iii. How sensitive are they to price, quality and service?
iv. Who has bought or expressed an interest in the product?

Describe your market:
i. How large is the market?
ii. How developed is the market and what is its history?
iii. What is the projected growth rate for the future?
iv. Identify unusual market characteristics such as barriers to entry.
v. What do published forecasts predict about the market's future?
vi. What is your market share?
vii. Are you aiming for particular market segments?
viii. What are your plans regarding export markets?

Discuss your company's competition:

i. What companies do you compete with?
ii. What are their strengths and weaknesses?
(Financial backing? Technology? Market share?)
iii. What are their similarities?
iv. What are their marketing strategies? Consider their likely response to your product.
v. Consider the potential for new competitors to enter the market
vi. Consider competition from overseas.

Section E – Marketing
Business Plan Content

Marketing Strategy

Set out your marketing strategy. Say if you are selling to a large or small number of customers and whether directly or through wholesalers or agents. Indicate how large a sales force you envisage. Discuss how you will identify and inform potential customers, and whether you will target any one group, and if so by sector or by geographical division. Elaborate on plans for advertising, direct mail or other promotional campaigns.

Say if your market is purely a domestic one, or whether there are opportunities for export sales. If so, describe these markets, the opportunities and the costs of operating overseas. Would you sell directly, license local manufacture or assembly or appoint local agents? Say how you would organise delivery, servicing and payment.

Finally, discuss the competition realistically. You have already acknowledged the challenge from their products. How do their marketing activities compare? From what you know of them, try to assess how they will react to your product or service, if it is a new or improved one. Consider also how easy it is for newcomers to enter the market – including rivals from abroad not yet competing in your marketplace.

Section E – Marketing
Business Plan Checklist

In this section you should make clear that you have a formulated **strategy** to achieve a reasonable share of the markets identified in Section D. Demonstrate that you understand the difference between 'Markets' and 'Marketing'. Describe the opportunities available in your market and show how your proposals will exploit them successfully. It will be helpful to prepare this section of the plan in parallel with Section D – Markets, since the two areas inevitably intertwine.

Recommendations
i.   Show that you have a clearly defined plan to achieve your sales goals.
ii. Show that you understand the concept of market positioning – critical Product/Service characteristics or uniqueness in relation to competitors.
iii. Develop a clear pricing policy; what margins do you require to be profitable and will the market bear this?
iv. Consider whether your product or service will require a distribution network or if direct selling is appropriate.
v.   Particularly in the case of a product, what is your field support policy?
vi. Consider the degree to which advertising and promotion is required to sell your product or service.
vii. Use marketing knowledge in the development of new products and/or services.

Key elements
Explain how you will achieve your sales goals:
i.   How will potential customers be identified?
ii. What customers will be the target in your initial marketing effort?
iii. Are advertising efforts important to your strategy?
iv. Consider the size of your sales force.

Demonstrate your market positioning strategy:
i.   What marketing strategy will you employ?
ii. What are the critical Product/Service characteristics?
iii. How is the Product/Service unique in relation to its competitors?
iv. How will you attract customers away from the competition?
v.   What is your pricing policy? Can you sell at margins which cover costs?

Show that you have a longer-term strategy for the business:
i.   Can you continue to sell direct to customers indefinitely?
ii. Will you, at some point, require a distribution network?
iii. Do you have a policy for dealing with customer queries and complaints?
iv. Have you thought about field support policy for your product?

Describe how you will use Marketing in the development of your Product/Service:
i.   Will you need formal accreditation to a Quality system standard such as ISO9000?
ii. Do you need to consider environmental issues in your business as set out in ISO14000?
iii. Have you considered the training needs of your employees, or even your own needs?
iv. Show how you will be market-driven, rather than product-driven, in developing your Product/Service.

Section F – Design/Development
Business Plan Content

Use this section when you have a technically complex product or service. If the product or service is not too sophisticated, this section can be ignored and the appropriate comments regarding development made in Section C.

Technology
State the stage of technical development the product has reached. Is it still on the drawing board, a working model, in production, or in use? Can the product range be expanded, and if so how, into what new areas and at what cost? If the purpose of raising money is to fund this activity, then highlight this aspect.

Touch upon both specific (to you) and general aspects of technical developments. What are your objectives and how much will new technology and technical advances affect what you plan? How important is research and development to your business, and what will you need to spend? How much of your resources, both financial and human, will this demand?

Technology Strategy
Develop a Technology Strategy for the business using the following plan:

1. Identify the appropriate unit for development.
2. State the main issues on the business strategic agenda.
3. Identify role of product features, product changes, process changes in the strategy.
4. Identify the specific technologies which the company is using/planning to use.
5. Identify technologies which the company might need in the medium term.
6. Map the technologies onto the products and services.
7. Assess extent to which particular technologies are central to competitive advantage.
8. Assess and re-think the company's strengths and weaknesses in all technologies.
9. Identify the major gaps or shortfalls (or over-resourcing) in the technologies.
10 Reflect on what steps might be taken to remedy the gaps.

Section F – Design/Development
Business Plan Checklist

Use this section only if your product or service is technically complex or is in need of considerable development work. Simpler or well-developed products and services can usually be dealt with in Section C.

Recommendations
i.   Demonstrate that you have a clearly defined Technology Strategy for the business.
ii.   Show that you have a clear understanding of your company's product(s) and that you have identified the needs for development.
iii. If development work is in progress, show that you have clearly identified its stage of development in the life-cycle of the product or service.
iv.   Evaluate the difficulties and risks in further development of the product/service and in bringing it to market.
v.   Describe how you will implement improvements in your product or service that you foresee or which will be demanded by your customers.
vi.   Consider how you will continue to develop your product or service to meet changing requirements in future markets.

Key elements
Explain your Technology Strategy for the business:
i.   Which technologies should be the basis of your business?
ii.   In which technologies should you become especially proficient?
iii. What distinctive technological competencies does your business require?
iv.   How should these competencies be embodied into products?
v.   Where should you obtain the requisite technology?
vi.   How much should you invest in technology development and how much should you purchase (the 'make v. buy' decision)?
vii. How should you organise and manage technology and innovation?
viii. When should the technology be introduced to the market?

Define your Research and Development policy:
i.   What are the future developments and objectives?
ii.   Discuss the influence of new technology.
iii. What are the technical risks?
iv.   Consider second and third generation products.

Section G – Manufacturing/Operations
Business Plan Content

How Will You Operate?

How does – or will – your business work from day to day? If you make things, this is where you describe the manufacturing process, premises, etc. If it is a retail business, describe the approach to merchandise, shop decor, display, hours of opening, etc. If it is a service activity, state what is involved in supplying that service.

As well as describing how the products are made, including details of components, ingredients, sub-assemblies, etc, say what the present production capacity is, how it could be increased, and at what capital or additional operating cost.

Identify the critical elements of the operation, for example the need to achieve high levels of quality, tight delivery deadlines and potential bottlenecks. Indicate key decisions that have to be made, including purchasing decisions. Say what relationships exist with suppliers.

Skills

State what skills are required, the availability of such skilled labour in your locality, and how you intend to attract and retain those people. Evaluate labour costs, including those of providing benefits, what trade unions are involved, and what industrial relations policies are followed or favoured.

Plant, Equipment, Premises

Itemise the important plant and equipment you either have, or will need to start or expand, giving costs. State what options are available including use of subcontractors if that is feasible. Talk about premises in a similar manner. Describe existing premises, and their location. Discuss their suitability now, and in the future, for your actual and projected needs. Will you need to move, or seek additional premises, and if so, when?

Section G – Manufacturing/Operations
Business Plan Checklist

This section should describe how your business will successfully and efficiently provide its product. For a manufacturing operation you should include a full description of the production process, the raw materials required and whether any particular trade skills are needed. For a service venture the availability of skilled personnel will be a prominent feature.

Recommendations
i.   Highlight any competitive advantages in your manufacturing/operations.
ii. Consider how you will manage the Supply Chain for your business.
iii. Describe how you will control your manufacturing/operations considering the need for computer-generated control systems.
iv. Show how you intend to handle the Procurement function in your business.

Key elements
Describe the production process:
i.   How will critical elements be controlled?
     (Bottlenecks? Quality? Delivery?)
ii. To what extent are you dependent on key factors – suppliers, materials, skilled labour?
iii. What make vs. buy decisions are involved?
iv. What raw materials are required?
v.   What is your relationship with suppliers?
vi. What is the production capacity? Is it sufficient for the future?

Discuss personnel requirements:
i.   What are your employee needs? Discuss any particular trade skills needed.
ii. What are your labour costs, including benefits?
iii. How will you attract sufficient, suitably qualified employees?
iv. What is the state of your industrial relations?
v.   Should you consider 'Investors in People' accreditation?

Evaluate your plant and equipment needs:
i.   What facilities and equipment needs?
ii. What future additions will be required for expansion and how much will they cost?

iii. Is there a need to rely on subcontractors?
iv. Do you need new state-of-the-art equipment or is reconditioned equipment adequate?

What are your needs for premises?
i. What are your existing premises and where are they located?
ii. Are your existing premises suitable for your needs?
iii. Do you need any additional premises?

What are your computer hardware/software requirements?
i. Do you have an Information Technology (IT) strategy?
ii. Have you evaluated the need for computer control systems?
iii. Do you need to consider local area or wide area networking systems?
iv. What general word and data processing software will you require?
v. Is your computer hardware adequately sized to meet you demands for the foreseeable future?
vi. What form of data storage are you considering?

Section H – Management
Business Plan Content

Who are the Management Team?

While business activities can alter dramatically, the leading personalities are less likely to change. It is the entrepreneur, and increasingly the management team, that matters most to those investing money.

This is where you start to sell the main asset you have to offer, that is the people with the ability to create and run a successful business. Start by describing the management structure. Be honest about deficiencies, stating what expertise you feel is or will be required to fill gaps.

List the main executives and their past record and achievements. Detailed resumés may be kept for an appendix. Try to show a good balance of expertise through the organisation. Say also what financial involvement they have, be it shares, options or profit-sharing bonuses, and the nature and length of service agreements or contracts, if they exist.

Mention the role of any outsiders, such as non-executive directors and consultants or advisers. Say which professionals – accountants, lawyers, bankers, etc – the company has engaged.

Refer to other key personnel, their terms of employment and what benefits and incentives are offered. State total numbers employed, including part-time staff, with a breakdown of skills and experience utilised, and discuss future recruitment plans.

Section H – Management
Business Plan Checklist

Investors will be particularly interested in the strength and quality of the management team, its background, experience and track record to date.

Recommendations
i.   Openly discuss the strengths and weaknesses of current management.
ii. Show what steps will be taken to rectify any weaknesses highlighted.
iii. Indicate what additional skills will be required as the venture grows.
iv. Include full profiles of key individuals and an organisation chart in appendices.

Key elements
Discuss the structure of the organisation:
i.   How are responsibilities distributed?
ii. Is management a one-man show?
iii. What additions to management are anticipated?
iv. Has any formal teamworking training/development taken place?

Identify key management personnel and their backgrounds:
i.   Who are the key managers and what have they accomplished in the past?
ii. What are their goals for the organisation?
iii. Is there a balance of skills among the members of management (marketing, research, finance, administration)?
iv. What steps have been taken to ensure that key members of the management team will be retained?
v.   Have any personal financial commitments been made to the business by the management team?

Describe the role of any outsiders in the venture:
i.   Are there to be any non-executives on the board of directors? What skills will they bring to the organisation?
ii. What professionals (lawyers, accountants, bankers) does the company rely upon?
iii. If no non-executive directors are envisaged, explain how you will deal with corporate governance issues and legislation arising from government reports such as Cadbury, Greenbury and Hampel.

Include general personnel details:

i.   Employment terms of key personnel
ii.   Planned staff numbers
iii.   Future recruitment plans
iv.   Other incentives issued to staff
v.   Qualifications and skills required.

Section J – Implementation Schedule
Business Plan Content

Timing

Timing is the essence, and this section helps to bring home the fact that you mean business. The plan describes something that is going to happen, and this shows potential investors when. It also indicates milestones and sets deadlines for you to meet.

Factors you should include are timings for:

i.   Obtaining finance
ii.   The capital expenditure programme
iii. Staff recruitment
iv. Product testing
v.   Contacting distributors
vi. Obtaining orders
vii. Production dates.

Section J – Implementation Schedule
Business Plan Checklist

The implementation schedule should outline all the activities required to implement the proposals set out in other sections of the Business Plan.

Key elements
The schedule should be internally consistent and co-ordinated with the financial projections and requests for finance (Section K). Typical factors should include timings for:
i.   Obtaining finance
ii. Capital expenditure programme
iii. Staff recruitment
iv. Product testing
v.   Contacting distributors
vi. Obtaining orders.

A timetable should indicate expected completion dates and milestones.

Decision points in the company's growth should be identified where the choice may be made to commit further funds.

Section K – Financial Highlights, Risks and Assumptions
Business Plan Content

How much Money will You Need?
However persuasive your outline, it has to be justified in figures. The finance section is where your numbers have to stand up and be counted.

Investors want to be assured that the figures are not just plausible back-of-an-envelope calculations, but have been carefully considered and prepared. Here, if nowhere else, is where you will need help from your accountants, unless you have a lot of financial experience.

Incorporated or Unincorporated
As described in Part I most requests for outside capital will require the formation of a limited company. However for smaller enterprises a sole trader or partnership will be preferred, especially at the initial stages. It is costly to maintain a company structure if you do not need to do so. It is also more likely that a personal tax regime will show advantages over company taxation.

A sole trader or partnership may still raise outside finance from family or friends and this is probably the way most individuals start out. In these circumstances it is essential that the terms set for the advance be clearly written down and copies retained by each party. The terms should include the amount, any security to be given, the rate of interest and the arrangements for repayment. If any of these are to be linked to performance then the basis of calculating profits and the share to be received by the outside investor needs to be clearly stated.

Partnerships
In the special case of a partnership it is usual for all partners to have rights as defined in a Partnership Agreement. This sets out the terms of handling partnership capital, which usually stays in the business, and partners' current accounts, to which are credited profits which can be drawn down as required. All partners are equally liable for the actions in the business of each other partner. Therefore it is essential that mutual trust is available between partners from the outset so that an equal sharing of risk is secured. An individual making a loan to a partnership needs to ensure that he has the terms of his relationship clearly defined in writing, otherwise he may be deemed to be a quasi-partner and liable if the business should fail.

Equity and Loan Capital

If a company structure is involved, first say in more detail how much money is required, and what it will be used for. Distinguish in broad terms between equity and loan capital. Equity is money invested in the business permanently; if the company fails the owners of the equity shareholdings lose their cash.

Equity share capital includes both ordinary and preference shares. Preference shares do not normally have voting rights, so do not dilute the level of management's control, but have rights over income and capital which rank ahead of the ordinary shares. There are many possible variations to the terms on which preference shares are issued so offering considerable flexibility in establishing an appropriate financing structure for a business.

Loan capital, as the name implies, is money lent to the business, perhaps for a fixed period. At some stage it is due to be repaid. Include also sources of other forms of finance, such as government grants and loans, hire-purchase agreements, etc.

Many investors may wish to split their investment between a mixture of loan and equity. Those kinds of details will be the subject of negotiation at a later date. They will be interested in the gearing, or ratio between loan and equity capital.

Personal Commitment

They will also want to know the personal involvement of you and your partners, all the more if it is a start-up or early-stage enterprise. You will have to demonstrate a commitment to the business in having something to lose and the incentive of having a lot to gain in building a strong and highly profitable concern.

If the business is already established, include here or as an appendix historical information, such as your latest audited accounts balance sheets, income statements and statements of sources and applications of funds – for the last two to five years.

Section K – Financial Highlights, Risks and Assumptions
Business Plan Checklist

If the business is in existence, the investor will want to assess your current financial position and you will need to provide your latest audited accounts, together with a commentary on the trends they reflect.

In any business, the investor will be interested in forecasts of profits and cash flow arising from the implementation of this Business Plan, incorporating the proposals detailed elsewhere in the other sections of the plan.

In addition, the amount and form of finance sought as well as a schedule for its repayment should be set out. Bear in mind that investors in start-up companies will want to see evidence of financial commitment on your part.

Recommendations
i.   Demonstrate the careful thought the financial projections have been given.
ii.   Document your assumptions explicitly.
iii. Include a detailed commentary on the financial projections.
iv.   Show that you have considered the risks inherent in the business; this may take the form of a 'sensitivity' or 'what if..?' analysis.
v.   Indicate how you will deal with the identified risks should they arise.
vi.   Give a summary of the important financial statements (Sales, Profits, Return on Capital, Net worth, etc.); this should not be a repetition of the detailed computer spreadsheets included in Section XI but present the highlights in easy-to-read form.

Key elements
Include historical statements.

Where possible, include full financial statements, balance sheets, income (profit & loss) statements, statements of sources and applications of funds for the past two to five years.

Present financial projections in summary form.

Prepare projected income (profit & loss) statements, balance sheets and cash flow statements for the next three to five years. These should be on a monthly basis for the first year and then quarterly. Include:
i.   Assumptions you have used in preparing the projections.
ii.   The impact of capital expenditure, fixed costs, and research and development costs on the cash flow.
iii. A break-even/sensitivity analysis, identifying the split between fixed and variable costs.
iv.   A contingency element, identified as such.

Section L – Detailed Financial Plan
Business Plan Content

Financial Projections

In presenting financial projections, prepare forecasts of income statements, balance sheets and cash flow statements for the next three to five years. For the first year, prepare these on a monthly basis, then quarterly thereafter.

Spell out the assumptions you have used in preparing the projections. You may decide that the difficulty of accurately predicting sales months and years ahead calls for two or more sets of assumptions – one optimistic, the other more conservative. You obviously then need two sets of projections. This is the kind of work computer spreadsheets were made for.

If you don't have the right equipment, or are unsure of how to go about it, call on your accountants. But don't include too many spreadsheets in your plan.

Investors don't want to be swamped by statistics. They want information that is clear and to the point. Let them see the likely impact on cash flow of capital expenditure, fixed and variable costs, and research and development costs.

Sensitivity Analyses

Also provide a break-even/sensitivity analysis. This can involve playing 'what-if' exercises on a computer, showing the effect varying assumptions will have on your projections. Identify the split between fixed and variable costs. Don't forget to include a reasonable contingency element, clearly identified as such.

Listing key ratios and industry standards will show outsiders how your kind of business should be judged in comparison to others in the same industry, as well as demonstrating your understanding of these problems. Ensure that the commentary on the figures fully explains what they mean, and that the sets of assumptions are clear to an outsider.

Section L – Detailed Financial Plan
Business Plan Checklist

This Section should consist of spreadsheets detailing the projected financial statements. It is often advisable to have these prepared by a qualified accountant who will know the format that the likely investor(s) will expect to see. Remember that you are the expert in your business and may well not be in accountancy; the potential investor may well be an expert in accountancy but will only rarely be an expert in your business.

If you do use an accountant in the preparation of these projections, always remember that this is **your** business; you must 'own' the numbers in the spreadsheets and be prepared to defend your assumptions and projections in discussions with the investor.

Recommendations
i.   Prepare the spreadsheets in accordance with the appropriate accounting procedures.
ii.   Check thoroughly that there are no transcription errors and that they are mutually compatible.
iii. Make sure that you have 'ownership' of the financial projections.

Key elements
Include the following, ideally in spreadsheet format:
i.   Profit and loss statements
ii.   Contribution and break-even analysis
iii. Cash flow analysis (monthly in first year)
iv.   Sensitivity analysis
v.   Balance sheets (annual only).

Section M – Appendices
Business Plan Content

We have pointed out a number of possible items that may warrant inclusion as an appendix. These should include documents that support or further explain strategies and policies expressed elsewhere in the plan. Don't introduce new information in this section.

As a checklist, here are some of the matters you may include:
i.   A glossary of technical terms, if appropriate
ii.   Profiles of key members of management
iii. Market research studies
iv.   Drawings and photographs of the product, premises, plant layout, etc
v.   Detailed technical specifications, patent applications, etc
vi.   A detailed organisation chart
vii. Legal documents, such as copies of contracts, agreements, leases, etc
viii. Letters of commitment from potential customers and suppliers
ix.   Copies of articles about your business and its operating environment.

Section M – Appendices
Business Plan Checklist

The appendices should include documentation which supports or further explains the strategies and observations noted elsewhere in the plan, for example:

i.   Profiles of key management personnel (track record, age, marital status, educational record, professional qualifications)
ii. Market research studies and/or consultant's reports
iii. Photographs or drawings of the product
iv. Detailed technical specifications
v.   Organisation chart (existing and proposed)
vi. Letters of commitment from potential customers and suppliers
vii. Order and/or Enquiry status
viii. Plant layout
ix. Contracts (e.g. management agreements, technology rights, leases, strategic alliances, supply chain partnerships)
x.   Magazine, newspaper and trade articles about your business and its operating environment.

New Business Guide
Part III – Endpiece

We have covered a lot of ground and much of it may be challenging. All of it will involve action of some sort. We have tried to make our approach both comprehensible and workable. Please do not be put off by those parts that may not apply to you personally. We are seeking to be inclusive but are also aware that this may come into the hands of some who are considering these matters from a perspective far removed from that of Western nations at the start of the Twenty-First Century. The good news is that starting a business has common features wherever you are in the world and at whatever stage of economic development that may surround you.

A Video Series
To demonstrate this point in practical fashion may we introduce you to an exciting project which has been launched by ICCC in parallel with the production of this book. ICCC was approached by the China Educational Television Service to make a series of video presentations on the subject 'You can start a business'. They cover much the same ground as this book but obviously in more depth. They also comprise a series of case studies from people from right across the world who have successfully applied these principles in their own businesses. Examples of this are a lady cake producer in Nigeria, a young toy manufacturer from Sri Lanka, a financial services expert from Singapore and a Chinese estate agent working in London. The variety of occupations, ethnic backgrounds, age groups and skills is truly amazing. The message conveyed to the Chinese students is that these gifts are for everyone. These videos were first shown on China TV in Spring 2000 and are scheduled for regular repeats.

You may be wondering why the China Educational Television Service are calling for the input of a Christian organisation for such a purpose. Well it is not to directly promote the Christian faith! It is because our calling is to serve and we do in fact have a unique economic message to convey. We are addressing a nation who for many years has experienced a closed society which resulted from a narrow interpretation of communism. Now their society is beginning to open up a place for a mixed economy with state and private enterprise working alongside each other. The skills of the market economy have to be re-learned and they are looking overseas for help.

However the problem with the free market economy as applied by many in the Western world is that it has become the tool of the God of Mammon – money and personal profit has become the ultimate goal. When this happens notions of service, fair prices, fair rewards and the care for customers, employees and the environment take a backward place. The system is refocused on self, engenders greed and ultimately would destroy our world.

The China Educational Television Service are wise in discerning that in our ICCC business practice we are defining not just an efficient economic process but a **way of life**. The Christian contribution is strong in this area and can help a nation come to terms with its past and assist in moulding the future. Many nations throughout the world will take heed of this.

The video series is currently available in Mandarin Russian and English. By the time you are reading this it will be available in many other languages. Business is universal, good business principles are universal and new businesses are being started in every part of the world in increasing measure. If you would like to purchase a video set for your own use please refer to Part IV.

Final Reminders
Having worked through the various sections of the book you will probably be in need of a rest. Before you relax may we add a few final observations and then send you on your way.

Any bias towards manufacture is because this usually involves more complex arrangements than for a service organisation. Even for a service company the requirement to find, train and install skilled labour will need careful analysis. Please do not be put off by what you may not need – concentrate on what you do need and skip the rest.

If you have found a bias towards standards and conditions operating in the UK and Western Europe please make the equivalent comparisons for standards, currencies and tax regulations within your own country. There are variations of practice but the principles will be the same because we now live in a global economy.

In all your financial planning recall that your sums must add up and you personally must own them. Ensure that sales less costs do equal net profit. Ensure that cash flow includes capital expenditure, is adjusted for timing differences and shows a realistic cash position. Ensure that your Balance Sheet shows the movements between Assets and Liabilities which themselves agree with the profits and cash flow that you are reporting. However, above all do not be ruled by figures. The narrative and assumptions you have made are just as important.

The Call

We started out by an analysis of the call to start a business. Having counted the cost now is the time not to feel discouraged but to commit yourself to start out on the way. The first step is always the most important. God is there to bring great support and encouragement for our endeavours. Millions throughout the world can give testimony to this. He would have you succeed in this project. Why not spend a moment in prayer affirming your intent to go forward in partnership with Him?

Part IV – References

The International Christian Chamber of Commerce can be reached through the International Office located in Sweden. The details are as follows:

ICCC Hjalmarbergets Forentagscenter
Mosavagen SE-702 Orebro
Sweden

Telephone +46 19 247 000

Fax +46 19 247 001

Web site www.iccc.net

The web site has links to Chambers in other parts of the world.

The ICCC in the United Kingdom and in Ireland can be reached through the national office located in Bristol UK. The details are as follows:

ICCC UK Office
79/81 Newfoundland Street
Bristol
BS2 9AP

Telephone +441179249754
Fax +441179249768

Email Office@uk.iccc.net

The authors of this publication can be reached by email at the following addresses:

Grahame Scofield   ghts@interalpha.co.uk
Ian Arbon   ian@enaineered-solutions.co.uk

See the web site for details of other relevant publications and magazines. They may be ordered online from the International Office.

There is a video series entitled 'You Can Start a Business' which was originally produced for China but which is now available in a number of languages.